AmblesideOnline Poetry Anthology Volume Three

William Blake
Sara Teasdale
Hilda Conkling
Helen Hunt Jackson

Edited and annotated by the AmblesideOnline Educational Foundation

AmblesideOnline Poetry Anthology Volume Three: William Blake, Sara Teasdale, Hilda Conkling, Helen Hunt Jackson
Copyright © 2021 by AmblesideOnline Educational Foundation

Cover design by Bryan White

ISBN: 9798453215973

Table of Contents

Introduction to the Series

Charlotte Mason said that poetry is an instructor of the conscience, and that children "must grow up upon the best... There is never a time when they are unequal to worthy thoughts, well put; inspiring tales, well told. Let Blake's 'Songs of Innocence' represent their standard in poetry..." and the result will be readers who demand the best, "the fit and beautiful expression of inspiring ideas and pictures of life" (*Parents and Children*, p. 263).

And modern research supports her claim. Researchers at the University of Liverpool found that reading poetry provides a "rocket-boost" to the brain that cannot be matched by straightforward, simple paraphrases. The research also found that poetry, in particular, "increased activity in the right hemisphere of the brain, an area concerned with 'autobiographical memory,' which helped the reader to reflect on and reappraise their own experiences in light of what they had read" (*Daily Mail*, Jan. 13, 2013).

AmblesideOnline students read a variety of poems which offer them word pictures and ideas to reflect on, and to help them interpret their own experiences.

> "[A student] should have practice, too, in reading aloud, for the most part, in the books he is using for his term's work. These should include a good deal of poetry, to accustom him to the delicate rendering of shades of meaning, and especially to make him aware that words are beautiful in themselves, that they are a source of pleasure, and are worthy of our honour; and that a beautiful word deserves to be beautifully said, with a certain roundness of tone and precision of utterance. Quite young children are open to this sort of teaching, conveyed, not in a lesson, but by a word now and then." (Charlotte Mason, *Home Education*, p. 227)

Please don't analyze and dissect these poems. There is time for that later in your young scholar's life. Just as there is a time to simply feed your young ones delicious, nourishing food, and a time later in their lives to teach them the analytical details of health, nutrition, and all about the vitamins and minerals in their food, there is a time to just read poetry and learn to enjoy it. "The thing is," Charlotte Mason said in a book she wrote for children, "to keep your eye upon words and wait to feel their force and beauty; and, when words are so fit that no other words can be put in their places, so few that none can be left out without spoiling the sense, and so fresh and musical that they delight you, then you may be sure that you are reading Literature, whether in prose or poetry. A great deal of delightful literature can be recognised only by this test." (*Ourselves Book I*, p. 41)

We hope you will enjoy reading these poems together as much as we enjoy sharing them with you.

An added note: we have tried to be sensitive to the changing language and ideas of our present day, while presenting these poems from the past as faithfully as we were able. However, it is beyond our capabilities to anticipate every new word meaning that exists or that arises in the future. We can only give the same advice and disclaimer that we would suggest for other studies, from literature through science: please preview this material, and then use it with care and discretion.

Donna-Jean Breckenridge
Lynn Bruce
Wendi Capehart
Karen Glass
Leslie Laurio
Anne White

Foreword to Volume Three

by Anne White

When I was a young child, our family owned an extra-large vintage tricycle. That tricycle made many trips up and down our block, sometimes tied to a wagon carrying another child or two. (I lived on the sort of school-reader block where children still played circus parade).

One night the tricycle was stolen from our front porch. (Obviously it wasn't the *perfect* school-reader block.) Since I was around six years old and seemingly too old for a tricycle, even a large one, my parents bought me a two-wheeled bicycle in its place. It was a lovely blue bicycle with a bell and a basket. However, like Elizabeth in Rumer Godden's book *The Fairy Doll*, I did not know how to ride a bicycle, and all the offered parental coaching did not seem enough to get me rolling.

So on went the training wheels, and they stayed on that bicycle an embarrassingly long time. Finally my younger sister was old enough to get her own two-wheeler, with a banana seat and high handlebars. And, wouldn't you know it, she immediately and literally began riding circles around me.

> "For a moment she wobbled; then she saw the silver
> wings filling and thrilling as they rushed through
> the air... 'Pedal. Pedal, pedal.'" (Rumer Godden, *The
> Fairy Doll*)

Although I did not have a Fairy Doll to ride on my handlebars, I decided that enough was enough, and that I would teach myself to ride a two-wheeler no matter what. The training wheels came off, and I suddenly realized that I did know what to do with my feet and the rest of me. Once in awhile I fell off, but so did everyone else.

Volume One of our Anthology might be considered a tricycle book (although it contains many poets who will be met again later on, so perhaps we can call it an extra-large tricycle). Volume Two, then, would be "training wheels." And Volume Three is for the time when one is big enough to ride without them, but not quite needing a bigger bike. Not just yet.

Volume Three is for a time when children are not too old for "Songs of Innocence," but just old enough to hear some "Songs of Experience." They can enjoy Blake's "songs of pleasant glee," and appreciate the simple imagery of Hilda Conkling's "Tree-toad is a leaf-gray shadow / That sings," and "The caterpillars, like little snow men, / Had wound themselves in their winter coats." But they can also wonder about Helen Hunt Jackson's "Songs which sang / Summer before no longer mean / The whole of summer," and mourn with her that it is "Too late to bid the violet live again. / The treachery, at last, too late, is plain." They can agree with Sara Teasdale that "life has loveliness to sell," but also feel the poignancy of Jackson's "They feel as if they were turning to stone, / They wish the neighbors would leave them alone."

Walk or run alongside, but don't push too hard during these years: your children will take off (and ask for bigger wheels) when they're ready.

In the meantime, here are Wendi Capehart's suggestions for making the most of this book.

How to Use These Poems with Young Students

It's really quite simple. Just read the poems aloud. One common approach is to read one poem a day, Monday through Thursday, and then, on Friday, ask if there are any previous poems the children would like to hear repeated.

You may also have your child read the daily poem aloud.

Or read it, casually, several times throughout the day, and see if your child doesn't start to pick up some of the poems.

Use a poem for copywork or transcription (handwriting practice).

Enjoy them. Don't dissect, analyze, parse, or otherwise drain them of their pleasure. All of those things are wonderful in their own time. But first, children (and parents) should just read lots of poems.

William Blake (1757-1827)

Biographical Sketch by Wendi Capehart and Leslie Laurio

William Blake was born in the Soho part of London on the 28th of November, 1757. His father, James Blake, kept a hosier's shop where he sold stockings. The family were not very well to do. Young William, a born individualist, was already marching to the beat of his own drum, although it meant he was often alone.

Even as a child, William Blake was clearly talented at design, and his father tried to do what he could to help his son realize his full potential. At the age of ten the boy was sent to a drawing school in the Strand (a part of London known as a place of entertainment, but which was also the home of many publishers and print shops). Meanwhile, William was cultivating his own artistic taste by constantly attending the different art sale rooms. He was strongly opinionated about what he liked, and was called "the little connoisseur." He began to collect printed copies of pictures by Michelangelo, Raphael, Dürer, and Heemskerk.

As a young man he was apprenticed to James Basire, a respected engraver, and he worked there for seven years. His apprenticeship had a great influence on his artistic education, and made him a skilled engraver. Almost all of his artistic output was in the form of engravings. At the end of his apprenticeship, he attended the school of the Royal Academy, where he continued his early study of antique art. Here, for the first time, he had the opportunity to draw from live models.

Not much is known of Blake's artistic education. We do not know if he ever systematically studied painting. He began using water colors on his own, and probably taught himself.

While he was still an apprentice, he married Catherine Boucher, the daughter of a market gardener who was his landlord and friend. He taught her to read and write, and trained her to engrave. She helped him to hand-color his illustrations throughout his life. They remained happily married until his death.

Blake had already become acquainted with some of the rising artists of his time, and now he began to meet literary people. At the Rev. Henry Mathew's home in Rathbone Place, he used to recite and sometimes sing poems he had written, and it was through the influence of Rev. Mathews that his first volume of poetry, called *Poetical Sketches*, was published in 1783.

William Blake had been educated as an engraver, but this book introduced him to the world as an artist who was also a gifted poet. He continued to publish his unique poems with his own original designs for the rest of his life.

In 1787, the *Songs of Innocence* were published. This book is remarkable for the beauty of both its verse and design, as well as the way the two were combined and expressed by the artist. Blake became his own printer and publisher. He engraved on copper, using a process he devised himself, and included engravings of both the text of his poems and the surrounding decorative design on the same plate. After the pages were printed from the copper plates, he colored them in by hand. Blake produced a work of fresh and living beauty in a way that had never been done before.

In spite of the distinct and beautiful quality of this book, it attracted very little attention. Perhaps that's not so surprising, considering the painstaking way in which it was created. But William Blake, never one to adapt himself to please the public, continued to produce other books of the same kind.

Blake was a stubborn individualist and visionary whose writings can't be judged by ordinary rules. The *Songs of Experience*, published in 1794 as a companion to the earlier *Songs of Innocence*, are mostly intelligible and coherent, but in these intervening works of "prophecy," as he called them, we see the first public glimpse of the part of his character and of his genius that made others wonder if he was completely sane. The question of whether Blake was or was not completely sane is still debated, but there is no doubt that he was sometimes under the influence of illusions that can't be explained. Much of his writing seems so unintelligible that there's no logical coherence. He clearly saw visions.

By 1796 Blake was actively employed as an illustrator. Richard Edwards, a bookseller in London, wanted to publish a new edition of Edward Young's *Night Thoughts*, and Blake was chosen to illustrate the work. The plan was to publish the work in nine parts, but only the first part, which including forty-three designs by Blake, was ever printed. These designs were engraved by Blake himself. Not only are they beautiful works of art in themselves, but Blake used his own peculiar system to associate each illustration with the text. Even today, the book is better known because of Blake's illustrations than for Young's poems.

Soon after the publication of this book, Blake was introduced to the poet William Hayley, and at Hayley's suggestion, he moved to Sussex. Hayley was planning to write a biography of William Cowper, and wanted Blake to illustrate it and keep him company. Blake lived in Sussex for three years. This was partly pleasant and partly inconvenient to Blake, and it apparently didn't help the progress of his art. One of the inconveniences was when he was tried for treason because of a rumor started by a soldier after Blake made him leave his garden. But even more inconvenient was his increasing irritation with William Hayley.

In 1804 Blake returned to London and began work on his most ambitious project—a book called *Jerusalem* which contained his own mythology mixed with his prophetic visions. He also worked on illustrations for The Book of Job.

He was working on prints to illustrate Dante's *Divine Comedy* when he died in 1827. When he saw his wife, Catherine, weeping at his bedside, he said to her, "Stay Kate! Keep just as you are—I will draw your portrait—for you have ever been an angel to me."

After William Blake died, his faithful wife continued to sell his artwork. She died four years later.

01. Piping down the valleys wild

Piping down the valleys wild,
Piping songs of pleasant glee,
On a cloud I saw a child,
And he laughing said to me:

'Pipe a song about a Lamb!'
So I piped with merry cheer.
'Piper, pipe that song again.'
So I piped: he wept to hear.

'Drop thy pipe, thy happy pipe;
Sing thy songs of happy cheer!'
So I sung the same again,
While he wept with joy to hear.

'Piper, sit thee down and write
In a book, that all may read.'
So he vanished from my sight;
And I plucked a hollow reed,

And I made a rural pen,
And I stained the water clear,
And I wrote my happy songs
Every child may joy to hear.

02. The Shepherd

How sweet is the shepherd's sweet lot!
From the morn to the evening he strays;
He shall follow his sheep all the day,
And his tongue shall be filled with praise.

For he hears the lambs' innocent call,
And he hears the ewes' tender reply;
He is watchful while they are in peace,
For they know when their shepherd is nigh.

03. The Echoing Green

The sun does arise,
And make happy the skies;
The merry bells ring
To welcome the Spring;
The skylark and thrush,
The birds of the bush,
Sing louder around
To the bells' cheerful sound;
While our sports shall be seen
On the echoing green.

Old John, with white hair,
Does laugh away care,
Sitting under the oak,
Among the old folk.
They laugh at our play,
And soon they all say,
'Such, such were the joys
When we all–girls and boys–
In our youth-time were seen
On the echoing green.'

Till the little ones, weary,
No more can be merry:
The sun does descend,
And our sports have an end.

Round the laps of their mothers
Many sisters and brothers,
Like birds in their nest,
Are ready for rest,
And sport no more seen
On the darkening green.

04. The Lamb

Little lamb, who made thee?
Dost thou know who made thee,
Gave thee life, and bid thee feed
By the stream and o'er the mead;
Gave thee clothing of delight,
Softest clothing, woolly, bright;
Gave thee such a tender voice,
Making all the vales rejoice?
Little lamb, who made thee?
Dost thou know who made thee?

Little lamb, I'll tell thee;
Little lamb, I'll tell thee:
He is called by thy name,
For He calls Himself a Lamb.
He is meek, and He is mild,
He became a little child.
I a child, and thou a lamb,
We are called by His name.
Little lamb, God bless thee!
Little lamb, God bless thee!

05. The Blossom

Merry, merry sparrow!
Under leaves so green
A happy blossom
Sees you, swift as arrow,
Seek your cradle narrow,
Near my bosom.
Pretty, pretty robin!
Under leaves so green
A happy blossom
Hears you sobbing, sobbing,
Pretty, pretty robin,
Near my bosom.

06. The Chimney Sweeper

When my mother died I was very young,
And my father sold me while yet my tongue
Could scarcely cry 'Weep! weep! weep! weep!'
So your chimneys I sweep, and in soot I sleep.

There's little Tom Dacre, who cried when his head,
That curled like a lamb's back, was shaved; so I said,
'Hush, Tom! never mind it, for, when your head's bare,
You know that the soot cannot spoil your white hair.'

And so he was quiet, and that very night,
As Tom was a-sleeping, he had such a sight! —
That thousands of sweepers, Dick, Joe, Ned, and Jack,
Were all of them locked up in coffins of black.

And by came an angel, who had a bright key,
And he opened the coffins, and set them all free;
Then down a green plain, leaping, laughing, they run
And wash in a river, and shine in the sun.

Then naked and white, all their bags left behind,
They rise upon clouds, and sport in the wind:
And the angel told Tom, if he'd be a good boy,
He'd have God for his father, and never want joy.

And so Tom awoke, and we rose in the dark,
And got with our bags and our brushes to work.
Though the morning was cold, Tom was happy and warm:
So, if all do their duty, they need not fear harm.

07. The Little Boy Lost

'Father, father, where are you going?
O do not walk so fast!
Speak, father, speak to your little boy,
Or else I shall be lost.'

The night was dark, no father was there,
The child was wet with dew;
The mire was deep, and the child did weep,
And away the vapour flew.

08. The Little Boy Found

The little boy lost in the lonely fen,
Led by the wandering light,
Began to cry, but God, ever nigh,
Appeared like his father, in white.

He kissed the child, and by the hand led,
And to his mother brought,
Who in sorrow pale, through the lonely dale,
Her little boy weeping sought.

09. Laughing Song

When the green woods laugh with the voice of joy,
And the dimpling stream runs laughing by;
When the air does laugh with our merry wit,
And the green hill laughs with the noise of it;

When the meadows laugh with lively green,
And the grasshopper laughs in the merry scene;
When Mary and Susan and Emily
With their sweet round mouths sing 'Ha ha he!'

When the painted birds laugh in the shade,
Where our table with cherries and nuts is spread:
Come live, and be merry, and join with me,
To sing the sweet chorus of 'Ha ha he!'

10. A Cradle Song

Sweet dreams, form a shade
O'er my lovely infant's head!
Sweet dreams of pleasant streams
By happy, silent, moony beams!

Sweet Sleep, with soft down
Weave thy brows an infant crown!
Sweet Sleep, angel mild,
Hover o'er my happy child!

Sweet smiles, in the night
Hover over my delight!
Sweet smiles, mother's smiles,
All the livelong night beguiles.

Sweet moans, dovelike sighs,
Chase not slumber from thy eyes!
Sweet moans, sweeter smiles,
All the dovelike moans beguiles.

Sleep, sleep, happy child!
All creation slept and smiled.
Sleep, sleep, happy sleep,
While o'er thee thy mother weep.

Sweet babe, in thy face
Holy image I can trace;
Sweet babe, once like thee
Thy Maker lay, and wept for me:

Wept for me, for thee, for all,
When He was an infant small.
Thou His image ever see,
Heavenly face that smiles on thee!

Smiles on thee, on me, on all,
Who became an infant small;
Infant smiles are His own smiles;
Heaven and earth to peace beguiles.

11. Holy Thursday

'Twas on a holy Thursday, their innocent faces clean,
The children walking two and two, in red, and blue, and green:
Grey-headed beadles walked before, with wands as white as snow,
Till into the high dome of Paul's they like Thames waters flow.

O what a multitude they seemed, these flowers of London town!
Seated in companies they sit, with radiance all their own.
The hum of multitudes was there, but multitudes of lambs,
Thousands of little boys and girls raising their innocent hands.

Now like a mighty wind they raise to heaven the voice of song,
Or like harmonious thunderings the seats of heaven among:
Beneath them sit the aged men, wise guardians of the poor.
Then cherish pity, lest you drive an angel from your door.

12. Night

The sun descending in the West,
The evening star does shine;
The birds are silent in their nest,
And I must seek for mine.
The moon, like a flower
In heaven's high bower,
With silent delight,
Sits and smiles on the night.

Farewell, green fields and happy groves,
Where flocks have took delight,
Where lambs have nibbled, silent moves
The feet of angels bright;
Unseen, they pour blessing,
And joy without ceasing,

On each bud and blossom,
And each sleeping bosom.

They look in every thoughtless nest
Where birds are covered warm;
They visit caves of every beast,
To keep them all from harm:
If they see any weeping
That should have been sleeping,
They pour sleep on their head,
And sit down by their bed.

When wolves and tigers howl for prey,
They pitying stand and weep;
Seeking to drive their thirst away,
And keep them from the sheep.
But, if they rush dreadful,
The angels, most heedful,
Receive each mild spirit,
New worlds to inherit.

And there the lion's ruddy eyes
Shall flow with tears of gold:
And pitying the tender cries,
And walking round the fold:
Saying: 'Wrath by His meekness,
And, by His health, sickness,
Is driven away
From our immortal day.

'And now beside thee, bleating lamb,
I can lie down and sleep,
Or think on Him who bore thy name,

Graze after thee, and weep.
For, washed in life's river,
My bright mane for ever
Shall shine like the gold,
As I guard o'er the fold.'

13. Spring

Sound the flute!
Now it's mute!
Birds delight,
Day and night,
Nightingale,
In the dale,
Lark in sky, —
Merrily,
Merrily, merrily to welcome in the year.

Little boy,
Full of joy;
Little girl,
Sweet and small;
Cock does crow,
So do you;
Merry voice,
Infant noise;
Merrily, merrily to welcome in the year.

Little lamb,
Here I am;
Come and lick
My white neck;

Let me pull
Your soft wool;
Let me kiss
Your soft face;
Merrily, merrily we welcome in the year.

14. Nurse's Song

When voices of children are heard on the green,
And laughing is heard on the hill,
My heart is at rest within my breast,
And everything else is still.
'Then come home, my children, the sun is gone down,
And the dews of night arise;
Come, come, leave off play, and let us away,
Till the morning appears in the skies.'

'No, no, let us play, for it is yet day,
And we cannot go to sleep;
Besides, in the sky the little birds fly,
And the hills are all covered with sheep.'
'Well, well, go and play till the light fades away,
And then go home to bed.'
The little ones leaped, and shouted, and laughed,
And all the hills echoed.

15. Infant Joy

'I have no name;
I am but two days old.'
What shall I call thee?
'I happy am,

Joy is my name.'
Sweet joy befall thee!

Pretty joy!
Sweet joy, but two days old.
Sweet joy I call thee:
Thou dost smile,
I sing the while;
Sweet joy befall thee!

16. A Dream

An emmet is an ant.

Once a dream did weave a shade
O'er my angel-guarded bed,
That an emmet lost its way
Where on grass methought I lay.

Troubled, wildered, and forlorn,
Dark, benighted, travel-worn,
Over many a tangled spray,
All heart-broke, I heard her say:

'O my children! do they cry,
Do they hear their father sigh?
Now they look abroad to see,
Now return and weep for me.'

Pitying, I dropped a tear:
But I saw a glow-worm near,
Who replied, 'What wailing wight
Calls the watchman of the night?'

'I am set to light the ground,
While the beetle goes his round:
Follow now the beetle's hum;
Little wanderer, hie thee home!'

17. On Another's Sorrow

Can I see another's woe,
And not be in sorrow too?
Can I see another's grief,
And not seek for kind relief?

Can I see a falling tear,
And not feel my sorrow's share?
Can a father see his child
Weep, nor be with sorrow filled?

Can a mother sit and hear
An infant groan, an infant fear?
No, no! never can it be!
Never, never can it be!

And can He who smiles on all
Hear the wren with sorrows small,
Hear the small bird's grief and care,
Hear the woes that infants bear—

And not sit beside the nest,
Pouring pity in their breast,
And not sit the cradle near,
Weeping tear on infant's tear?

And not sit both night and day,
Wiping all our tears away?
O no! never can it be!
Never, never can it be!

He doth give His joy to all:
He becomes an infant small,
He becomes a man of woe,
He doth feel the sorrow too.

Think not thou canst sigh a sigh,
And thy Maker is not by:
Think not thou canst weep a tear,
And thy Maker is not near.

O He gives to us His joy,
That our grief He may destroy:
Till our grief is fled and gone
He doth sit by us and moan.

18. from *Songs of Experience*

Hear the voice of the Bard,
Who present, past, and future, sees;
Whose ears have heard
The Holy Word
That walked among the ancient trees;

Calling the lapsed soul,
And weeping in the evening dew;
That might control
The starry pole,
And fallen, fallen light renew!

'O Earth, O Earth, return!
Arise from out the dewy grass!
Night is worn,
And the morn
Rises from the slumbrous mass.

'Turn away no more;
Why wilt thou turn away?
The starry floor,
The watery shore,
Is given thee till the break of day.'

19. Earth's Answer

Earth raised up her head
From the darkness dread and drear,
Her light fled,
Stony, dread,
And her locks covered with grey despair.

'Prisoned on watery shore,
Starry jealousy does keep my den
Cold and hoar;
Weeping o'er,
I hear the father of the ancient men.

'Selfish father of men!
Cruel, jealous, selfish fear!
Can delight,
Chained in night,
The virgins of youth and morning bear.

'Does spring hide its joy,
When buds and blossoms grow?
Does the sower
Sow by night,
Or the ploughman in darkness plough?

'Break this heavy chain,
That does freeze my bones around!
Selfish, vain,
Eternal bane,
That free love with bondage bound.'

20. The Clod and the Pebble

'Love seeketh not itself to please,
Nor for itself hath any care,
But for another gives its ease,
And builds a heaven in hell's despair.'

So sung a little clod of clay,
Trodden with the cattle's feet,
But a pebble of the brook
Warbled out these metres meet:

'Love seeketh only Self to please,
To bind another to its delight,
Joys in another's loss of ease,
And builds a hell in heaven's despite.'

21. The Fly

Little Fly,
Thy summer's play
My thoughtless hand
Has brushed away.

Am not I
A fly like thee?
Or art not thou
A man like me?

For I dance,
And drink, and sing,
Till some blind hand
Shall brush my wing.

If thought is life
And strength and breath,
And the want
Of thought is death;

Then am I
A happy fly.
If I live,
Or if I die.

22. The Tyger

Tyger, tyger, burning bright
In the forests of the night,
What immortal hand or eye
Could frame thy fearful symmetry?

In what distant deeps or skies
Burnt the fire of thine eyes?
On what wings dare he aspire?
What the hand dare seize the fire?

And what shoulder and what art
Could twist the sinews of thy heart?
And, when thy heart began to beat,
What dread hand and what dread feet?

What the hammer? what the chain?
In what furnace was thy brain?
What the anvil? what dread grasp
Dare its deadly terrors clasp?

When the stars threw down their spears,
And watered heaven with their tears,
Did He smile His work to see?
Did He who made the lamb make thee?

Tyger, tyger, burning bright
In the forests of the night,
What immortal hand or eye
Dare frame thy fearful symmetry?

23. My Pretty Rose Tree

A flower was offered to me,
Such a flower as May never bore;
But I said, 'I've a pretty rose tree,'
And I passed the sweet flower o'er.

Then I went to my pretty rose tree,
To tend her by day and by night;
But my rose turned away with jealousy,
And her thorns were my only delight.

24. The Lily

The modest Rose puts forth a thorn,
The humble sheep a threat'ning horn:
While the Lily white shall in love delight,
Nor a thorn nor a threat stain her beauty bright.

25. A Cradle Song

Sleep, sleep, beauty bright,
Dreaming in the joys of night;
Sleep, sleep; in thy sleep
Little sorrows sit and weep.

Sweet babe, in thy face
Soft desires I can trace,
Secret joys and secret smiles,
Little pretty infant wiles.

As thy softest limbs I feel,
Smiles as of the morning steal
O'er thy cheek, and o'er thy breast
Where thy little heart doth rest.

O the cunning wiles that creep
In thy little heart asleep!
When thy little heart doth wake,
Then the dreadful light shall break.

From thy cheek and from thy eye
O'er the youthful harvest nigh
Infant wiles and infant smiles
Heaven and Earth of peace beguiles.

26. The Schoolboy

I love to rise in a summer morn,
When the birds sing on every tree;
The distant huntsman winds his horn,
And the skylark sings with me:
O! what sweet company!

But to go to school in a summer morn, —
O! it drives all joy away!
Under a cruel eye outworn,
The little ones spend the day
In sighing and dismay.

Ah! then at times I drooping sit,
And spend many an anxious hour;
Nor in my book can I take delight,
Nor sit in learning's bower,
Worn through with the dreary shower.

How can the bird that is born for joy
Sit in a cage and sing?
How can a child, when fears annoy,
But droop his tender wing,
And forget his youthful spring!

O father and mother if buds are nipped,
And blossoms blown away;
And if the tender plants are stripped
Of their joy in the springing day,
By sorrow and care's dismay, —

How shall the summer arise in joy,
Or the summer fruits appear?
Or how shall we gather what griefs destroy,
Or bless the mellowing year,
When the blasts of winter appear?

27. Eternity

He who binds to himself a joy
Does the winged life destroy;
But he who kisses the joy as it flies
Lives in eternity's sun rise.

28. From Auguries of Innocence

To see a world in a grain of sand
And a heaven in a wild flower,
Hold infinity in the palm of your hand
And eternity in an hour.

A robin redbreast in a cage
Puts all Heaven in a rage.
A dove house fill'd with doves and pigeons
Shudders Hell thro' all its regions.

A dog starv'd at his master's gate
Predicts the ruin of the state.

A horse misus'd upon the road
Calls to Heaven for human blood.

Each outcry of the hunted hare
A fibre from the brain does tear.
A skylark wounded in the wing,
A Cherubim does cease to sing.

The game cock clipp'd and arm'd for fight
Does the rising Sun affright.
Every wolf's and lion's howl
Raises from Hell a human soul.

He who respects the infant's faith
Triumphs over Hell and Death.
The child's toys and the old man's reasons
Are the fruits of the two seasons.

The questioner, who sits so sly,
Shall never know how to reply.
He who replies to words of doubt
Doth put the light of Knowledge out.

29. Degrade first the Arts

Degrade first the Arts if you'd Mankind Degrade.
Hire Idiots to Paint with cold light and hot shade:
Give high Price for the worst, leave the best in disgrace,
And with Labours of Ignorance fill every place.

30. from The Two Songs

I heard an Angel Singing
When the day was springing:
"Mercy, pity, and peace,
Are the world's release."

So he sang all day
Over the new-mown hay,
Till the sun went down,
And the haycocks looked brown.

31. The Wild Flower's Song

As I wander'd in the forest,
The green leaves among,
I heard a wild flower
Singing a song:

"I slept in the earth
In the silent night,
I murmur'd my thoughts
And I felt delight.

In the morning I went
As rosy as morn
To seek for new joy,
But I met with scorn."

32. The Fairy

'Come hither, my Sparrows,
My little arrows.
If a tear or a smile

Will a man beguile,
If an amorous delay
Clouds a sunshiny day,
If the step of a foot
Smites the heart to its root,
'Tis the marriage ring . . .
Makes each fairy a king.'

So a fairy sung.
From the leaves I sprung;
He leap'd from the spray
To flee away;
But in my hat caught,
He soon shall be taught.
Let him laugh, let him cry,
He's my Butterfly;
For I've pull'd out the sting
Of the marriage-ring.

33. To Spring

O thou, with dewy locks, who lookest down
Thro' the clear windows of the morning; turn
Thine angel eyes upon our western isle,
Which in full choir hails thy approach, O Spring!

The hills tell each other, and the list'ning
Vallies hear; all our longing eyes are turned
Up to thy bright pavillions: issue forth,
And let thy holy feet visit our clime.

Come o'er the eastern hills, and let our winds
Kiss thy perfumed garments; let us taste

Thy morn and evening breath; scatter thy pearls
Upon our love-sick land that mourns for thee.

O deck her forth with thy fair fingers; pour
Thy soft kisses on her bosom; and put
Thy golden crown upon her languish'd head,
Whose modest tresses were bound up for thee!

34. To Summer

O thou, who passest thro' our vallies in
Thy strength, curb thy fierce steeds, allay the heat
That flames from their large nostrils! thou, O Summer,
Oft pitched'st here thy golden tent, and oft
Beneath our oaks hast slept, while we beheld
With joy, thy ruddy limbs and flourishing hair.

Beneath our thickest shades we oft have heard
Thy voice, when noon upon his fervid car
Rode o'er the deep of heaven; beside our springs
Sit down, and in our mossy vallies, on
Some bank beside a river clear, throw thy
Silk draperies off, and rush into the stream:
Our vallies love the Summer in his pride.

Our bards are fam'd who strike the silver wire:
Our youth are bolder than the southern swains:
Our maidens fairer in the sprightly dance:
We lack not songs, nor instruments of joy,
Nor echoes sweet, nor waters clear as heaven,
Nor laurel wreaths against the sultry heat.

35. To Autumn

O Autumn, laden with fruit, and stained
With the blood of the grape, pass not, but sit
Beneath my shady roof, there thou may'st rest,
And tune thy jolly voice to my fresh pipe;
And all the daughters of the year shall dance!
Sing now the lusty song of fruits and flowers.

"The narrow bud opens her beauties to
The sun, and love runs in her thrilling veins;
Blossoms hang round the brows of Morning, and
Flourish down the bright cheek of modest Eve,
Till clust'ring Summer breaks forth into singing,
And feather'd clouds strew flowers round her head.

"The spirits of the air live on the smells
Of fruit; and Joy, with pinions light, roves round
The gardens, or sits singing in the trees."
Thus sang the jolly Autumn as he sat;
Then rose, girded himself, and o'er the bleak
Hills fled from our sight; but left his golden load.

36. To Winter

Adamantine means unbreakable.

O Winter! bar thine adamantine doors:
The north is thine; there hast thou built thy dark
Deep-founded habitation. Shake not thy roofs,
Nor bend thy pillars with thine iron car.

He hears me not, but o'er the yawning deep
Rides heavy; his storms are unchain'd; sheathed

In ribbed steel, I dare not lift mine eyes;
For he hath rear'd his sceptre o'er the world.

Lo! now the direful monster, whose skin clings
To his strong bones, strides o'er the groaning rocks:
He withers all in silence, and his hand
Unclothes the earth, and freezes up frail life.

He takes his seat upon the cliffs, the mariner
Cries in vain. Poor little wretch! that deal'st
With storms; till heaven smiles, and the monster
Is driv'n yelling to his caves beneath mount Hecla.

37. To the Evening Star

Thou fair-hair'd angel of the evening,
Now, while the sun rests on the mountains, light
Thy bright torch of love; thy radiant crown
Put on, and smile upon our evening bed!
Smile on our loves; and, while thou drawest the
Blue curtains of the sky, scatter thy silver dew
On every flower that shuts its sweet eyes
In timely sleep. Let thy west wind sleep on
The lake; speak silence with thy glimmering eyes,
And wash the dusk with silver. Soon, full soon,
Dost thou withdraw; then the wolf rages wide,
And the lion glares thro' the dun forest:
The fleeces of our flocks are cover'd with
Thy sacred dew: protect them with thine influence.

38. To Morning

O holy virgin! clad in purest white,
Unlock heav'n's golden gates, and issue forth;
Awake the dawn that sleeps in heaven; let light
Rise from the chambers of the east, and bring
The honied dew that cometh on waking day.
O radiant morning, salute the sun,
Rouz'd like a huntsman to the chace; and, with
Thy buskin'd feet, appear upon our hills.

39. Jerusalem

*In 1804, we are told, William Blake had gotten himself into political trouble and
was accused of treason. While awaiting his trial, he worked on a poem called Preface
to Milton (he had been working on a longer poem about the poet John Milton).
Observing some of the unhappy situations of his time, such as the dirty mills and
factories of the Industrial Revolution, he thought of an old folk story, that Jesus had
visited England when he was young. If Jesus should come there in Blake's own time,
he wondered, would he make it a happier, more beautiful place? And even if he did
not, what if the people themselves could work together to restore justice and beauty
to their land?*

*Years later, Blake's poem was set to music, and it became a favorite hymn of
the English people. It is often called "Jerusalem."*

And did those feet in ancient time
Walk upon England's mountains green:
And was the holy Lamb of God,
On England's pleasant pastures seen!

And did the Countenance Divine,
Shine forth upon our clouded hills?
And was Jerusalem builded here,
Among these dark Satanic Mills?

Bring me my Bow of burning gold:
Bring me my arrows of desire:
Bring me my Spear: O clouds unfold!
Bring me my Chariot of fire!

I will not cease from Mental Fight,
Nor shall my sword sleep in my hand:
Till we have built Jerusalem,
In England's green and pleasant Land.

40. I Love the Jocund Dance

I love the jocund dance,
The softly breathing song,
Where innocent eyes do glance,
And where lisps the maiden's tongue.

I love the laughing vale,
I love the echoing hill,
Where mirth does never fail,
And the jolly swain laughs his fill.

I love the pleasant cot,
I love the innocent bow'r,
Where white and brown is our lot,
Or fruit in the mid-day hour.

I love the oaken seat,
Beneath the oaken tree,
Where all the old villagers meet,
And laugh our sports to see.

Blake

I love our neighbours all,
But, Kitty, I better love thee;
And love them I ever shall;
But thou art all to me.

This is another of Blake's poems that Wordsworth copied into his commonplace book.

Sara Teasdale (1884-1933)

Biographical Sketch by Leslie Laurio

Sara Teasdale was born into a well-to-do family in St. Louis, Missouri. Even as a child, she loved pretty things. In fact, her first word was "pretty." Her three much older siblings doted on their little sister, whom they affectionately called "Sadie," and treated like a princess. She was homeschooled until age ten due to frail health, and lived an extremely sheltered life. She grew up believing she was delicate and helpless, and that perception never left her. It caused her anxiety and made her feel very dependent on others. Yet she was often left alone and had to amuse herself because her siblings were so much older, and she had no peers. Because her family considered her delicate, she was not allowed to run around and play like most children. She was a shy and lonely child.

She went to a private girls' school where she made friends and began to write, both poetry and prose. As a young woman, she joined a group of other young women artists in St. Louis who called themselves The Potters and published a magazine called *The Potter's Wheel*.

She was a fan of an Italian actress named Eleonora Duse, and, although they never met, Sara wrote poems in her honor. Those poems became her first book–*Sonnets to Duse*–and brought her recognition in the literary world.

When she was 21, Sara went on a tour of Europe, Egypt, and the Holy Land with her mother. She was captivated by the architecture. Shortly after they returned, Sara's health deteriorated and she spent five lonely months at a sanitarium in Connecticut to recover.

Many young men were interested in Sara. The poet Vachel Lindsay proposed to her, but she turned him down and married a businessman named Ernst Filsinger, and moved with him to New York. Ernst loved Sara deeply and was very devoted to her, but he traveled a lot, and she was left alone much of the time —just as she had been as a child. Sara was an emotional person, frequently depressed, often unwell, and very dependent. She decided marriage was not for her and after fifteen years, she divorced Ernst. Ernst was broken-hearted. They had no children. Sara devoted the rest of her life to her work. She wrote poems, and edited books of poems by other poets, including the children's collection *Rainbow Gold*, dedicated to her father, as well as a book of poems by female poets.

Her poetry is lyrical, almost musical, and as finely crafted as a polished jewel. Her book *Rivers to the Sea* (1918), was praised by the *New York Times Book Review* as "a little volume of joyous and unstudied song." Reviewers compared her to Christina Rossetti, William Blake, and A. E. Housman. Her poems were admired by other poets for their delicate simplicity. Her book *Love Songs* was chosen by Columbia University as 1917's best book of poetry, before Pulitzer Prizes were given for poetry.

But in spite of her success, anxiety, depression, and frail health continued to plague her. One of her brothers had been paralyzed by a stroke and spent twenty years in a wheelchair. Sara feared suffering the same fate. She had taken a trip to Europe to research a biography she wanted to write about Christina Rossetti, and came back to New York with a nasty bout of pneumonia. Before she was fully recovered, a blood vessel burst in her hand. She was convinced that she was having a stroke. Despondent at the thought of becoming paralyzed, she took her own life at the age of forty-eight.

In addition to the poems we have been able to include here, her book *Stars To-night: Verses for Boys and Girls* (1930) contains these poems: Night, Late October, The Falling Star, The Spicebush in March, Calm Morning at Sea, A June Day, Rhyme of November Stars, I Stood Upon a Star, Winter Noon, February Twilight. The book is out of print but worth attempting to locate. Some of its individual poems, like February Twilight and The Falling Star, can be found by doing a search online.

01. The Love that Goes A-begging

from *Sonnets to Duse*, 1907

Oh Loves there are that enter in,
And Loves there are that wait,
And Loves that sit a-weeping
Whose joy will come too late.

For some there be that ope their doors,
And some there be that close,
And Love must go a-begging,
But whither, no one knows.

02. Wishes

from *Sonnets to Duse*, 1907

I wish for such a lot of things
That never will come true —
And yet I want them all so much
I think they might, don't you?
I want a little kitty-cat
That's soft and tame and sweet,
And every day I watch and hope
I'll find one in the street.

But nursie says, "Come, walk along,
"Don't stand and stare like that" —
I'm only looking hard and hard
To try to find my cat.

And then I want a blue balloon
That tries to fly away,

I thought if I wished hard enough
That it would come some day.

One time when I was in the park
I knew that it would be
Beside the big old clock at home
A-waiting there for me —

And soon as we got home again,
I hurried thro' the hall,
And looked beside the big old clock —
It wasn't there at all.

I think I'll never wish again —
But then, what shall I do?
The wishes are a lot of fun
Altho' they don't come true.

03. Dusk in Autumn

from *Sonnets to Duse*, 1907

A scimitar is a short sword with a curved blade.

The moon is like a scimitar,
A little silver scimitar,
A-drifting down the sky.
And near beside it is a star,
A timid twinkling golden star,
That watches like an eye.

And thro' the nursery window-pane
The witches have a fire again,

Just like the ones we make, —
And now I know they're having tea,
I wish they'd give a cup to me,
With witches' currant cake.

04. Dream Song

from *Sonnets to Duse*, 1907

I plucked a snow-drop in the spring,
And in my hand too closely pressed;
The warmth had hurt the tender thing,
I grieved to see it withering.

I gave my love a poppy red,
And laid it on her snow-cold breast;
But poppies need a warmer bed,
We wept to find the flower was dead.

05. Faults

from *Sonnets to Duse*, 1907

They came to tell your faults to me,
They named them over one by one,
I laughed aloud when they were done;
I knew them all so well before, —
Oh they were blind, too blind to see
Your faults had made me love you more.

06. Snow Song

from *Helen of Troy and Other Poems*, 1911

Fairy snow, fairy snow,
Blowing, blowing everywhere,
Would that I
Too, could fly
Lightly, lightly through the air.

07. November

from *Helen of Troy and Other Poems*, 1911

The world is tired, the year is old,
The little leaves are glad to die,
The wind goes shivering with cold
Among the rushes dry.

08. A Winter Night

from *Helen of Troy and Other Poems*, 1911

My window-pane is starred with frost,
The world is bitter cold to-night,
The moon is cruel and the wind
Is like a two-edged sword to smite.

God pity all the homeless ones,
The beggars pacing to and fro.
God pity all the poor to-night
Who walk the lamp-lit streets of snow.

09. Dawn

from *Helen of Troy and Other Poems*, 1911

The greenish sky glows up in misty reds,
The purple shadows turn to brick and stone,
The dreams wear thin, men turn upon their beds,
And hear the milk-cart jangle by alone.

10. Dusk

from *Helen of Troy and Other Poems*, 1911

The city's street, a roaring blackened stream
Walled in by granite, thro' whose thousand eyes
A thousand yellow lights begin to gleam,
And over all the pale untroubled skies.

11. Rain at Night

from *Helen of Troy and Other Poems*, 1911

The street-lamps shine in a yellow line
Down the splashy, gleaming street,
And the rain is heard now loud now blurred
By the tread of homing feet.

12. A Ballad of Two Knights

from *Helen of Troy and Other Poems*, 1911

Two knights rode forth at early dawn
A-seeking maids to wed,

Said one, "My lady must be fair,
With gold hair on her head."

Then spake the other knight-at-arms:
"I care not for her face,
But she I love must be a dove
For purity and grace."

13. The Faery Forest

from *Helen of Troy and Other Poems*, 1911

The faery forest glimmered
Beneath an ivory moon,
The silver grasses shimmered
Against a faery tune.

Beneath the silken silence
The crystal branches slept,
And dreaming thro' the dew-fall
The cold white blossoms wept.

14. A Minuet of Mozart's

from *Helen of Troy and Other Poems*, 1911

Across the dimly lighted room
The violin drew wefts of sound,
Airily they wove and wound
And glimmered gold against the gloom.

I watched the music turn to light,
But at the pausing of the bow,

The web was broken and the glow
Was drowned within the wave of night.

15. Twilight

from *Helen of Troy and Other Poems*, 1911

Dreamily over the roofs
The cold spring rain is falling,
Out in the lonely tree
A bird is calling, calling.

Slowly over the earth
The wings of night are falling;
My heart like the bird in the tree
Is calling, calling, calling.

16. Grandfather's Love

from *Helen of Troy and Other Poems*, 1911

They said he sent his love to me,
They wouldn't put it in my hand,
And when I asked them where it was
They said I couldn't understand.

I thought they must have hidden it,
I hunted for it all the day,
And when I told them so at night
They smiled and turned their heads away.

They say that love is something kind,
That I can never see or touch.

I wish he'd sent me something else,
I like his cough-drops twice as much.

17. The Kind Moon

from *Helen of Troy and Other Poems*, 1911

I think the moon is very kind
To take such trouble just for me.
He came along with me from home
To keep me company.

He went as fast as I could run;
I wonder how he crossed the sky?
I'm sure he hasn't legs and feet
Or any wings to fly.

Yet here he is above their roof;
Perhaps he thinks it isn't right
For me to go so far alone,
Tho' mother said I might.

18. Spring Night

from *Rivers to the Sea*, 1915

The park is filled with night and fog,
The veils are drawn about the world,
The drowsy lights along the paths
Are dim and pearled.

Gold and gleaming the empty streets,
Gold and gleaming the misty lake,

The mirrored lights like sunken swords,
Glimmer and shake.

Oh, is it not enough to be
Here with this beauty over me?
My throat should ache with praise, and I
Should kneel in joy beneath the sky.
Oh, beauty, are you not enough?

19. April

from Rivers to the Sea, 1915

The roofs are shining from the rain,
The sparrows twitter as they fly,
And with a windy April grace
The little clouds go by.

Yet the back yards are bare and brown
With only one unchanging tree —
I could not be so sure of Spring
Save that it sings in me.

20. A Winter Blue Jay

from Rivers to the Sea, 1915

Crisply the bright snow whispered,
Crunching beneath our feet;
Behind us as we walked along the parkway,
Our shadows danced,
Fantastic shapes in vivid blue.
Across the lake the skaters
Flew to and fro,

With sharp turns weaving
A frail invisible net.
In ecstasy the earth
Drank the silver sunlight;
In ecstasy the skaters
Drank the wine of speed;
In ecstasy we laughed
Drinking the wine of love.
Had not the music of our joy
Sounded its highest note?
But no,

For suddenly, with lifted eyes you said,
"Oh look!"
There, on the black bough of a snow flecked maple,
Fearless and gay as our love,
A bluejay cocked his crest!
Oh who can tell the range of joy
Or set the bounds of beauty?

21. In the Train

from *Rivers to the Sea*, 1915

Fields beneath a quilt of snow
From which the rocks and stubble sleep,
And in the west a shy white star
That shivers as it wakes from deep.

The restless rumble of the train,
The drowsy people in the car,
Steel blue twilight in the world,
And in my heart a timid star.

22. Morning

from *Rivers to the Sea*, 1915

I went out on an April morning
All alone, for my heart was high,
I was a child of the shining meadow,
I was a sister of the sky.

There in the windy flood of morning
Longing lifted its weight from me,
Lost as a sob in the midst of cheering,
Swept as a sea-bird out to sea.

23. May Night

from *Rivers to the Sea*, 1915

The spring is fresh and fearless
And every leaf is new,
The world is brimmed with moonlight,
The lilac brimmed with dew.

Here in the moving shadows
I catch my breath and sing
My heart is fresh and fearless
And over-brimmed with spring.

24. Dusk in June

from *Rivers to the Sea*, 1915

Evening, and all the birds
In a chorus of shimmering sound

Are easing their hearts of joy
For miles around.

The air is blue and sweet,
The few first stars are white,
Oh let me like the birds
Sing before night.

25. The Sea Wind

from *Rivers to the Sea*, 1915

I am a pool in a peaceful place,
I greet the great sky face to face,
I know the stars and the stately moon
And the wind that runs with rippling shoon
But why does it always bring to me
The far-off, beautiful sound of the sea?

The marsh-grass weaves me a wall of green,
But the wind comes whispering in between,
In the dead of night when the sky is deep
The wind comes waking me out of sleep
Why does it always bring to me
The far-off, terrible call of the sea?

26. The Cloud

from *Rivers to the Sea*, 1915

I am a cloud in the heaven's height,
The stars are lit for my delight,
Tireless and changeful, swift and free,
I cast my shadow on hill and sea

But why do the pines on the mountain's crest
Call to me always, "Rest, rest"?

I throw my mantle over the moon
And I blind the sun on his throne at noon,
Nothing can tame me, nothing can bind,
I am a child of the heartless wind
But oh the pines on the mountain's crest
Whispering always, "Rest, rest."

27. The Star

from *Rivers to the Sea*, 1915

A white star born in the evening glow
Looked to the round green world below,
And saw a pool in a wooded place
That held like a jewel her mirrored face.
She said to the pool: "Oh, wondrous deep,
I love you, I give you my light to keep.
Oh, more profound than the moving sea
That never has shown myself to me!
Oh, fathomless as the sky is far,
Hold forever your tremulous star!"

But out of the woods as night grew cool
A brown pig came to the little pool;
It grunted and splashed and waded in
And the deepest place but reached its chin.
The water gurgled with tender glee
And the mud churned up in it turbidly.
The star grew pale and hid her face
In a bit of floating cloud like lace.

28. In the Carpenter's Shop

from *Rivers to the Sea*, 1915

Mary sat in the corner dreaming,
Dim was the room and low,
While in the dusk, the saw went screaming
To and fro.

Jesus and Joseph toiled together,
Mary was watching them,
Thinking of kings in the wintry weather
At Bethlehem.

Mary sat in the corner thinking,
Jesus had grown a man;
One by one her hopes were sinking
As the years ran.

Jesus and Joseph toiled together,
Mary's thoughts were far
Angels sang in the wintry weather
Under a star.

Mary sat in the corner weeping,
Bitter and hot her tears
Little faith were the angels keeping
All the years.

29. Swallow Flight

from *Rivers to the Sea*, 1915

I love my hour of wind and light,
I love men's faces and their eyes,
I love my spirit's veering flight
Like swallows under evening skies.

30. Thoughts

from *Rivers to the Sea*, 1915

When I can make my thoughts come forth
To walk like ladies up and down,
Each one puts on before the glass
Her most becoming hat and gown.

But oh, the shy and eager thoughts
That hide and will not get them dressed,
Why is it that they always seem
So much more lovely than the rest?

31. To Dick on his Sixth Birthday

from *Rivers to the Sea*, 1915

Tho' I am very old and wise,
And you are neither wise nor old,
When I look far into your eyes,
I know things I was never told:
I know how flame must strain and fret
Prisoned in a mortal net;
How joy with over-eager wings,

Bruises the small heart where he sings;
How too much life, like too much gold,
Is sometimes very hard to hold....
All that is talking but I know
This much is true, six years ago
An angel living near the moon
Walked thru the sky and sang a tune
Plucking stars to make his crown
And suddenly two stars fell down,
Two falling arrows made of light.
Six years ago this very night

I saw them fall and wondered why
The angel dropped them from the sky
But when I saw your eyes I knew
The angel sent the stars to you.

32. To Rose

from *Rivers to the Sea*, 1915

Rose, when I remember you,
Little lady, scarcely two,
I am suddenly aware
Of the angels in the air.

All your softly gracious ways
Make an island in my days
Where my thoughts fly back to be
Sheltered from too strong a sea.

All your luminous delight
Shines before me in the night

When I grope for sleep and find
Only shadows in my mind.

Rose, when I remember you,
White and glowing, pink and new,
With so swift a sense of fun
Altho' life has just begun;

With so sure a pride of place
In your very infant face,
I should like to make a prayer
To the angels in the air:
"If an angel ever brings
Me a baby in her wings,
Please be certain that it grows
Very, very much like Rose."

33. Night in Arizona

from *Rivers to the Sea*, 1915

The moon is a charring ember
Dying into the dark;
Off in the crouching mountains
Coyotes bark.

The stars are heavy in heaven,
Too great for the sky to hold —
What if they fell and shattered
The earth with gold?

No lights are over the mesa,
The wind is hard and wild,

I stand at the darkened window
And cry like a child.

34. Vignettes Overseas: Stresa

from *Rivers to the Sea*, 1915

The moon grows out of the hills
A yellow flower,
The lake is a dreamy bride
Who waits her hour.

Beauty has filled my heart,
It can hold no more,
It is full, as the lake is full,
From shore to shore.

35. Barter

from *Rivers to the Sea*, 1915

Life has loveliness to sell
All beautiful and splendid things,
Blue waves whitened on a cliff,
Soaring fire that sways and sings,
And children's faces looking up
Holding wonder like a cup.

Life has loveliness to sell,
Music like a curve of gold,
Scent of pine trees in the rain,
Eyes that love you, arms that hold,
And for your spirit's still delight,
Holy thoughts that star the night.

Spend all you have for loveliness,
Buy it and never count the cost;
For one white singing hour of peace
Count many a year of strife well lost,
And for a breath of ecstasy
Give all you have been, or could be.

36. Stars

from Flame and Shadow, 1920

Alone in the night
On a dark hill
With pines around me
Spicy and still,

And a heaven full of stars
Over my head,
White and topaz
And a misty red;

Myriads with beating
Hearts of fire
That aeons
Cannot vex or tire;

Up the dome of heaven
Like a great hill,
I watch them marching
Stately and still,

And I know that I
Am honored to be

Witness
Of so much majesty.

37. The Coin

from *Flame and Shadow*, 1920

Into my heart's treasury
I slipped a coin
That time cannot take
Nor a thief purloin, —
Oh, better than the minting
Of a gold-crowned king
Is the safe-kept memory
Of a lovely thing.

38. May Day

from *Flame and Shadow*, 1920

A delicate fabric of bird song
Floats in the air,
The smell of wet wild earth
Is everywhere.
Red small leaves of the maple
Are clenched like a hand,
Like girls at their first communion
The pear trees stand.

Oh I must pass nothing by
Without loving it much,
The raindrop try with my lips,
The grass with my touch;

For how can I be sure
I shall see again
The world on the first of May
Shining after the rain?

39. Thoughts

from *Flame and Shadow*, 1920

When I am all alone
Envy me most,
Then my thoughts flutter round me
In a glimmering host;

Some dressed in silver,
Some dressed in white,
Each like a taper
Blossoming light;

Most of them merry,
Some of them grave,
Each of them lithe
As willows that wave;

Some bearing violets,
Some bearing bay,
One with a burning rose
Hidden away —

When I am all alone
Envy me then,
For I have better friends
Than women and men.

Hilda Conkling (1910-1986)

"[Children]... have the singular faculty of being able
to make concrete images out of the merest gossamer
of a fairy tale. A seven year old child sings, —

> I cannot see fairies,
> I dream them.
> There is no fairy that can hide from me;
> I keep on dreaming till I find him.
> There you are, Primrose! I see you,
Blackwing!"

(Charlotte Mason, *Philosophy of Education*, p. 210)

"Fairy Gifts": Biographical Sketch by Anne White

One day when Hilda Conkling was about ten years old, she went to see a movie with her friends. In those days, silent picture shows began with a newsreel, which showed all kinds of world events and interesting happenings. When the newsreel began, Hilda was horrified to see her own face on the screen. "I could have died," she recalled later, "when the other children started pointing and laughing." What made a ten-year-old girl so newsworthy? She had been "writing" poetry since the age of four; she was now the author of *Poems by a Little Girl*, and she would go on to publish two more books before "retiring" in her early teens.

Many of us have read about composers, athletes, actors, and others whose talents were apparent very early in their lives. Some of them, like Mozart, seem to have been pushed into their careers by overly-eager parents. Others were treated more like Handel, who (as we are told by one of his biographers), was forbidden by his father to play any music, but practiced secretly in the attic. Sometimes child prodigies turn out to have long, successful careers, like the cellist Yo-Yo Ma. Some cannot cope with the pressure (or their decreasing fame), and

57

get themselves into trouble. But others simply walk away from their gifts, and are discovered years later selling insurance or raising cattle. What was Hilda Conkling's story?

Hilda and her older sister Elsa were raised in Massachusetts by their mother, Grace Hazard Conkling, who was a professor of English and had many literary acquaintances, including Robert Frost and Walter de la Mare. Hilda's parents divorced when she was very young, and for that reason and others, she had an extremely close relationship with her mother. The foreword to *Poems*, which was written by the poet Amy Lowell, makes it sound as if they led quite an idyllic life:

> "The children and their mother live all the year
> round in Northampton, and glimpses of the woods
> and hills surrounding the little town crop up again
> and again in these poems. This is Emily Dickinson's
> country, and there is a reminiscent sameness in the
> fauna and flora of her poems in these. The two little
> girls go to a school a few blocks from where they
> live. In the afternoons, they take long walks with
> their mother, or play in the garden while she writes.
> On rainy days, there are books and Mrs. Conkling's
> piano, which is not just a piano, for Mrs. Conkling is
> a musician..."

Preschooler Hilda, according to one source, was first overheard "telling" original bits of poetry to an imaginary friend. Her mother suggested that Hilda "tell her poems" to her instead, and this was the way that all of the poems were recorded, often without Hilda's awareness.

> "I didn't realize mother was writing down what I
> said," she said. "She wrote poems, too, and always
> had a pad in her hands, so it didn't seem unusual,
> me babbling, her scribbling. But later, she'd read
> them back to me, and I always knew if she'd taken a
> word down wrong, I could always correct her."

This unusual way of working caused accusations that Grace Conkling was in fact the author of Hilda's poems; but they both denied this, and Amy Lowell's essay, overly cheerful as it may be, does seem to prove that it was Hilda's own imagination that created them.

What happened to make Hilda stop creating poems? Again, it seems to have been a suggestion of her mother's which, this time, had unfortunate consequences. After the publication of Hilda's second book of poems (the third was a compilation of the first two), Grace Conkling asked her to begin writing them down for herself.

But she never did.

Some commenters have suggested that Hilda had some form of learning disability that made writing difficult for her. However, the fact that she went on to study at good schools (paid for with the royalties from her books), that she taught children and then managed bookstores for most of her life makes it clear that this wasn't a woman who avoided books; and in an interview years later, she never suggested such a thing. What is obvious, though, is that Hilda's mother was a dominant force in her life, from childhood until Grace's death in 1958. It seems just as likely that, without her mother as her audience and secretary, Hilda simply lost her motivation to write. Hilda herself said that, rather than encouraging her to find her voice as an adult poet, her mother seemed to downplay her talents. Perhaps this was because she wanted her daughter to enjoy a "normal" sort of life, without the embarrassing media attention she had already received. However, Hilda said that her mother's message that "you are just like everyone else" caused her to grow up not quite knowing what to do with herself. "I wasn't knocking myself out," she later admitted.

Hilda Conkling never married, and continued to live in the same area for the rest of her life. She thought about writing an autobiography, and said that she sometimes "thought" bits of poetry, but if she did write any of it down, it was never published. She lived in an apartment with several cats, and died at the age of seventy-five.

But for those few years when Hilda's "fairy gift" was hers to use, she was, as Amy Lowell said,

> "possessed of a rare and accurate power of
> observation. And when we add this to her gift of
> imagination, we see that it is the perfectly natural
> play of these two faculties which makes what to her
> is an obvious expression... By this means, her
> poetical gift has functioned happily, without ever
> for a moment experiencing the tension of doubt."

01. Moon Song

There is a star that runs very fast,
That goes pulling the moon
Through the tops of the poplars.
It is all in silver,
The tall star:
The moon rolls goldenly along
Out of breath.
Mr. Moon, does he make you hurry?

02. Chickadee

The chickadee in the appletree
Talks all the time very gently.
He makes me sleepy.
I rock away to the sea-lights.
Far off I hear him talking
The way smooth bright pebbles
Drop into water . . .
Chick-a-dee-dee-dee . . .

03. Red Rooster

Red rooster in your gray coop,
O stately creature with tail-feathers red and blue,
Yellow and black,
You have a comb gay as a parade
On your head:
You have pearl trinkets
On your feet:
The short feathers smooth along your back
Are the dark color of wet rocks,
Or the rippled green of ships

When I look at their sides through water.
I don't know how you happened to be made
So proud, so foolish,
Wearing your coat of many colors,
Shouting all day long your crooked words,
Loud . . . sharp . . . not beautiful!

04. Tree Toad

Tree-toad is a small gray person
With a silver voice.
Tree-toad is a leaf-gray shadow
That sings.
Tree-toad is never seen
Unless a star squeezes through the leaves,
Or a moth looks sharply at a gray branch.
How would it be, I wonder,
To sing patiently all night,
Never thinking that people are asleep?
Raindrops and mist, starriness over the trees,
The moon, the dew, the other little singers,
Cricket . . . toad . . . leaf rustling . . .
They would listen:
It would be music like weather
That gets into all the corners
Of out-of-doors.

Every night I see little shadows
I never saw before.
Every night I hear little voices
I never heard before.
When night comes trailing her starry cloak,
I start out for slumberland,

With tree-toads calling along the roadside.
Good-night, I say to one, Good-by, I say to another:
I hope to find you on the way
We have traveled before!
I hope to hear you singing on the Road of Dreams!

05. Dandelion

O little soldier with the golden helmet,
What are you guarding on my lawn?
You with your green gun
And your yellow beard,
Why do you stand so stiff?
There is only the grass to fight!

06. Little Snail

I saw a little snail
Come down the garden walk.
He wagged his head this way . . . that way . . .
Like a clown in a circus.
He looked from side to side
As though he were from a different country.
I have always said he carries his house on his back . . .
To-day in the rain
I saw that it was his umbrella!

07. The Old Bridge

The old bridge has a wrinkled face.
He bends his back
For us to go over.
He moans and weeps
But we do not hear.

Sorrow stands in his face
For the heavy weight and worry
Of people passing.
The trees drop their leaves into the water;
The sky nods to him.
The leaves float down like small ships
On the blue surface
Which is the sky.
He is not always sad:
He smiles to see the ships go down
And the little children
Playing on the river banks.

08. Gift

This is mint and here are three pinks
I have brought you, Mother.
They are wet with rain
And shining with it.
The pinks smell like more of them
In a blue vase:
The mint smells like summer
In many gardens.

09. I Am

I am willowy boughs
For coolness;
I am gold-finch wings
For darkness;
I am a little grape
Thinking of September,
I am a very small violet
Thinking of May.

10. Spring Song

I love daffodils.
I love Narcissus when he bends his head.
I can hardly keep March and spring and Sunday and daffodils
Out of my rhyme of song.
Do you know anything about the spring
When it comes again?
God knows about it while winter is lasting.
Flowers bring him power in the spring,
And birds bring it, and children.
He is sometimes sad and alone
Up there in the sky trying to keep his worlds happy.
I bring him songs
When he is in his sadness, and weary.
I tell him how I used to wander out
To study stars and the moon he made,
And flowers in the dark of the wood.
I keep reminding him about his flowers he has forgotten,
And that snowdrops are up.
What can I say to make him listen?
"God," I say,
"Don't you care!
Nobody must be sad or sorry
In the spring-time of flowers."

11. Water

The world turns softly
Not to spill its lakes and rivers.
The water is held in its arms
And the sky is held in the water.

What is water,
That pours silver,
And can hold the sky?

12. Autumn Song

I made a ring of leaves
On the autumn grass:
I was a fairy queen all day.
Inside the ring, the wind wore sandals
Not to make a noise of going.
The caterpillars, like little snow men,
Had wound themselves in their winter coats.
The hands of the trees were bare
And their fingers fluttered.
I was a queen of yellow leaves and brown,
And the redness of my fairy ring
Kept me warm.
For the wind blew near,
Though he made no noise of going,
And I hadn't a close-made wrap
Like the caterpillars.
Even a queen of fairies can be cold
When summer has forgotten and gone!
Keep me warm, red leaves;
Don't let the frost tiptoe into my ring
On the magic grass!

13. Thunder Shower

The dark cloud raged.
Gone was the morning light.
The big drops darted down:
The storm stood tall on the rose-trees:

And the bees that were getting honey
Out of wet roses,
The hiding bees would not come out of the flowers
Into the rain.

14. Purple Asters

It isn't alone the asters
In my garden,
It is the butterflies gleaming
Like crowns of kings and queens!
It isn't alone purple
And blue on the edge of purple,
It is what the sun does,
And the air moving clearly,
The petals moving and the wings,
In my queer little garden!

15. Moon Thought

The moon is thinking of the river
Winding through the mountains far away,
Because she has a river in her heart
Full of the same silver.

16. Sun Flowers

Sun-flowers, stop growing!
If you touch the sky where those clouds are passing
Like tufts of dandelion gone to seed,
The sky will put you out!
You know it is blue like the sea . . .

Maybe it is wet, too!
Your gold faces will be gone forever
If you brush against that blue
Ever so softly!

17. Poplars

The poplars bow forward and back;
They are like a fan waving very softly.
They tremble,
For they love the wind in their feathery branches.
They love to look down at the shallows,
At the mermaids
On the sandy shore;
They love to look into morning's face
Cool in the water.

18. Fairies

I cannot see fairies.
I dream them.
There is no fairy can hide from me;
I keep on dreaming till I find him:
There you are, Primrose! I see you, Black Wing!

19. Snowflake Song

Snowflakes come in fleets
Like ships over the sea.
The moon shines down on the crusty snow:
The stars make the sky sparkle like gold-fish
In a glassy bowl.
Bluebirds are gone now,

But they left their song behind them.
The moon seems to say:
It is time for summer when the birds come back
To pick up their lonesome songs.

20. Snowstorm

Snowflakes are dancing.
They run down out of heaven.
Coming home from somewhere down the long tired road
They flake us sometimes
The way they do the grass,
And the stretch of the world.
The grass-blades are crowned with snowflakes.
They make me think of daisies
With white frills around their necks
With golden faces and green gowns;
Poor little daisies,
Tip-toe and shivering
In the cold!

21. Poppy

Oh big red poppy,
You look stern and sturdy,
Yet you bow to the wind
And sing a lullaby . . .
"Sleep, little ones under my breast
In the moonshine . . ."
You make this lullaby,
Sweet, short,
Slow, beautiful,
And you thank the dew for giving you a drink.

22. Clouds

The clouds were gray all day.
At last they departed
And the blue diamonds shone again.
I watched clouds float past and flow back
Like waves across the sea,
Waves that are foamy and soft,
When they hear clouds calling
Mother Sea, send us up your song
Of hushaby!

23. Humming-Bird

Why do you stand on the air
And no sun shining?
How can you hold yourself so still
On raindrops sliding?
They change and fall, they are not steady,
But you do not know they are gone.
Is there a silver wire
I cannot see?
Is the wind your perch?
Raindrops slide down your little shoulders . . .
They do not wet you:
I think you are not real
In your green feathers!
You are not a humming-bird at all
Standing on air above the garden!
I dreamed you the way I dream fairies,
Or the flower I lost yesterday!

Helen Hunt Jackson (1830-1885)

Biographical Sketch by Donna-Jean Breckenridge

Once I discovered Helen Hunt Jackson, the opening months of our school years were not complete without the poem that included these lines:

> "By all these lovely tokens
> September days are here,
> With summer's best of weather,
> And autumn's best of cheer."

Since I always felt rather sad at the conclusion of summer, her words - and a trip to the apple orchard – helped make the seasonal transition a little easier.

And the next month always involved reciting this gem from Jackson, usually on a day we picked pumpkins:

> "O suns and skies and clouds of June,
> And flowers of June together,
> Ye cannot rival for one hour
> October's bright blue weather."

But as wonderful as those two poems are, there is so much more to this poet.

Helen Hunt Jackson, one of the best-known authors of her time, was born Helen Maria Fiske in 1830 in Amherst, Massachusetts. Yes, she was born the same year, in the same town, as another famous poet, Emily Dickinson. Their warm friendship, though, did not deepen until later in both their lives.

Helen was the daughter of a minister. Her mother died when she was 13, and her father followed in death just a few years later. When Helen was 22, she married Edward Hunt, a captain in the U.S. Corps of Engineers. Their baby boy, Murray, was born a year later —but he died at the age of eleven months, from a brain disease.

A year after that heartbreak, their second son Warren ("Rennie") was born. The Civil War broke out, and two years into the war, Helen's husband Edward was killed during an experiment. Two years later, in 1865, Helen's beloved son Rennie died of diphtheria, at the age of 9.

Helen was overwhelmed with grief. But it was not long before that grief was directed into writing. In the aftermath of the Civil War and its massive losses, no doubt many could share in her pain. In her haunting poem "The Prince is Dead," she writes these words:

> "They dare not look where the cradle is set;
> They hate the sunbeam which is set on the
> floor,
> But will make the baby laugh out no more;
> They feel as if they were turning to stone,
> They wish the neighbors would leave them
> alone.
> The Prince is dead."

And in her poem "Best," she writes,

> "Mother, I see you, with your nursery light,
> Leading your babies, all in white,
> To their sweet rest;
> Christ, the Good Shepherd, carries mine to-
> night,
> And that is best."

As Helen began to travel to Europe and throughout the United States, she began to write on a variety of topics. Ralph Waldo Emerson called her "America's greatest woman poet."

But Helen was not well, and her doctor advised her to go to Colorado, to avail herself of the clear air. Once in Colorado, Helen met and married William Sharpless Jackson (throughout her life, Helen objected to being called Helen Hunt Jackson. She said that a woman does not identify herself by the names of both of her husbands).

While visiting her sister back east one day, Helen heard a speech by a man from the Ponca tribe, named Chief Standing Bear. He talked about things the United States government had done against his people, about broken promises, and about the government taking their land and forcing them onto reservations.

Helen turned her writing towards the cause of Native people. She wrote a nonfiction book called "A Century of Dishonor." That book talked about the injustice that Native people had suffered. But it was her next book, a work of fiction, that moved people powerfully. The book was entitled *Ramona*, and it was meant to be a sympathetic telling of the problems Native people faced. Though her expressions are different than those we use today, we can appreciate Helen's sympathy toward Native people. Referring to the impact of the novel *Uncle Tom's Cabin* on the emancipation of the slaves, she wrote, "If I can do one-hundredth part for the Indian that Mrs. Stowe did for the Negro, I will be thankful."

In 1885, the year after *Ramona* was published, Helen fell and broke her hip. Later that year, she died of cancer, at the age of 55.

In a letter of sympathy to Helen's husband, Emily Dickinson related this last exchange from Helen: "Dear friend, can you walk, were the last words that I wrote her. I can fly—her immortal (soaring) reply."

01. The Way to Sing

The birds must know. Who wisely sings
    Will sing as they;
The common air has generous wings.
    Songs make their way.
No messenger to run before,
    Devising plan;
No mention of the place or hour
    To any man;
No waiting till some sound betrays
    A listening ear;
No different voice, no new delays,
    If steps draw near.

What bird is that? Its song is good.
    And eager eyes
Go peering through the dusky wood,
    In glad surprise.
Then late at night, when by his fire
    The traveller sits,
Watching the flame grow brighter, higher,
    The sweet song flits
By snatches through his weary brain
    To help him rest;
When next he goes that road again,
    An empty nest
On leafless bough will make him sigh,
    Ah me! last spring
Just here I heard, in passing by,
    That rare bird sing!

But while he sighs, remembering
    How sweet the song,
The little bird on tireless wing,
    Is borne along
In other air, and other men
    With weary feet,
On other roads, the simple strain
    Are finding sweet.
The birds must know. Who wisely sings
    Will sing as they;
The common air has generous wings,
    Songs make their way.

02. Outward Bound

The hour has come. Strong hands the anchor raise;
Friends stand and weep along the fading shore,
In sudden fear lest we return no more,
In sudden fancy that he safer stays
Who stays behind; that some new danger lays
New snare in each fresh path untrod before.
Ah, foolish hearts! In fate's mysterious lore
Is written no such choice of plan and days:
Each hour has its own peril and escape;
In most familiar things' familiar shape
New danger comes without or sight or sound;
No sea more foreign rolls than breaks each morn
Across our thresholds when the day is born:
We sail, at sunrise, daily, "outward bound."

03. God's Light-Houses

When night falls on the earth, the sea
  From east to west lies twinkling bright
With shining beams from beacons high
  Which flash afar a friendly light.

The sailor's eyes, like eyes in prayer,
  Turn unto them for guiding ray:
If storms obscure their radiance,
  The great ships helpless grope their way.

When night falls on the earth, the sky
  Looks like a wide, a boundless main.
Who knows what voyagers sail there?
  Who names the ports they seek and gain?

Are not the stars like beacons set
  To guide the argosies that go
From universe to universe,
  Our little world above, below?—

On their great errands solemn bent,
  In their vast journeys unaware
Of our small planet's name or place
  Revolving in the lower air.

O thought too vast! O thought too glad!
  An awe most rapturous it stirs.
From world to world God's beacons shine:
  God means to save his mariners!

04. Morning-Glory

Wondrous interlacement!
Holding fast to threads by green and silky rings,
With the dawn it spreads its white and purple wings;
Generous in its bloom, and sheltering while it clings
　　Sturdy morning-glory.
　　Creeping through the casement,
Slanting to the floor in dusty, shining beams,
Dancing on the door in quick, fantastic gleams,
Comes the new day's light, and pours in tideless streams,
　　Golden morning-glory.
　　In the lowly basement,
Rocking in the sun, the baby's cradle stands;
Now the little one thrusts out his rosy hands;
Soon his eyes will open; then in all the lands
　　No such morning-glory!

05. September

The golden-rod is yellow;
　The corn is turning brown;
The trees in apple orchards
　With fruit are bending down.

The gentian's bluest fringes
　Are curling in the sun;
In dusty pods the milkweed
　Its hidden silk has spun.

The sedges flaunt their harvest,
　In every meadow nook;
And asters by the brook-side
　Make asters in the brook,

From dewy lanes at morning
  The grapes' sweet odors rise;
At noon the roads all flutter
  With yellow butterflies.

By all these lovely tokens
  September days are here,
With summer's best of weather,
  And autumn's best of cheer.

But none of all this beauty
  Which floods the earth and air
Is unto me the secret
  Which makes September fair.

'T is a thing which I remember;
  To name it thrills me yet:
One day of one September
  I never can forget.

06. October's Bright Blue Weather

O suns and skies and clouds of June,
  And flowers of June together,
Ye cannot rival for one hour
  October's bright blue weather;

When loud the bumblebee makes haste,
  Belated, thriftless vagrant,
And goldenrod is dying fast,
  And lanes with grapes are fragrant;

When gentians roll their fingers tight
  To save them for the morning,
And chestnuts fall from satin burrs
  Without a sound of warning;

When on the ground red apples lie
  In piles like jewels shining,
And redder still on old stone walls
  Are leaves of woodbine twining;

When all the lovely wayside things
  Their white-winged seeds are sowing,
And in the fields still green and fair,
  Late aftermaths are growing;

When springs run low, and on the brooks,
  In idle golden freighting,
Bright leaves sink noiseless in the hush
  Of woods, for winter waiting;

When comrades seek sweet country haunts,
  By twos and twos together,
And count like misers, hour by hour,
  October's bright blue weather.

O sun and skies and flowers of June,
  Count all your boasts together,
Love loveth best of all the year
  October's bright blue weather.

07. Chance

These things I wondering saw beneath the sun:
That never yet the race was to the swift,
The fight unto the mightiest to lift,
Nor favors unto men whose skill had done
Great works, nor riches ever unto one
Wise man of understanding. All is drift
Of time and chance, and none may stay or sift
Or know the end of that which is begun.
Who waits until the wind shall silent keep,
Will never find the ready hour to sow.
Who watcheth clouds will have no time to reap.
At daydawn plant thy seed, and be not slow
At night. God doth not slumber take nor sleep:
Which seed shall prosper thou canst never know.

08. "Down to Sleep."

November woods are bare and still;
November days are clear and bright;
Each noon burns up the morning's chill;
The morning's snow is gone by night;
Each day my steps grow slow, grow light,
As through the woods I reverent creep,
Watching all things lie "down to sleep."

I never knew what beds,
Fragrant to smell, and soft to touch,
The forest sifts and shapes and spreads;
I never knew before how much
Of human sound there is in such
Low tones as through the forest sweep
When all wild things lie "down to sleep."

Each day I find new coverlids
Tucked in, and more sweet eyes shut tight;
Sometimes the viewless mother bids
Her ferns kneel down, full in my sight;
I hear their chorus of "good-night;"
And half I smile, and half I weep,
Listening while they lie "down to sleep."

November woods are bare and still;
November days are bright and good;
Life's noon burns up life's morning chill;
Life's night rests feet which long have stood;
Some warm soft bed, in field or wood,
The mother will not fail to keep,
Where we can "lay us down to sleep."

09. My Strawberry

O marvel, fruit of fruits, I pause
To reckon thee. I ask what cause
Set free so much of red from heats
At core of earth, and mixed such sweets
With sour and spice: what was that strength
Which out of darkness, length by length,
Spun all thy shining thread of vine,
Netting the fields in bond as thine.
I see thy tendrils drink by sips
From grass and clover's smiling lips;
I hear thy roots dig down for wells,
Tapping the meadow's hidden cells;
   Whole generations of green things,
Descended from long lines of springs,

I see make room for thee to bide
A quiet comrade by their side;
I see the creeping peoples go
Mysterious journeys to and fro,
Treading to right and left of thee,
Doing thee homage wonderingly.
I see the wild bees as they fare,
Thy cups of honey drink, but spare.
I mark thee bathe and bathe again
In sweet uncalendared spring rain.
I watch how all May has of sun
Makes haste to have thy ripeness done,
While all her nights let dews escape
To set and cool thy perfect shape.
Ah, fruit of fruits, no more I pause
To dream and seek thy hidden laws!
I stretch my hand and dare to taste,
In instant of delicious waste
On single feast, all things that went
To make the empire thou hast spent.

10. Joy

O Joy, hast thou a shape?
    Hast thou a breath?
How fillest thou the soundless air?
Tell me the pillars of thy house
What rest they on? Do they escape
    The victory of Death?
And are they fair
    Eternally, who enter in thy house?
O Joy, thou viewless spirit, canst thou dare
    To tell the pillars of thy house?

On adamant of pain,
  Before the earth
Was born of sea, before the sea,
Yea, and before the light, my house
Was built. None know what loss, what gain,
  Attends each travail birth.
No soul could be
  At peace when it had entered in my house,
If the foundations it could touch or see,
  Which stay the pillars of my house!

11. Dedication

When children in the summer weather play,
Flitting like birds through sun and wind and rain
From road to field, from field to road again,
Pathetic reckoning of each mile they stray
They leave in flowers forgotten by the way;
Forgotten, dying, but not all in vain,
Since, finding them, with tender smiles, half pain,
Half joy, we sigh, "Some child passed here to-day."
Dear one, —whose name I name not lest some tongue
Pronounce it roughly, —like a little child
Tired out at noon, I left my flowers among
The wayside things. I know how thou hast smiled,
And that the thought of them will always be
One more sweet secret thing 'twixt thee and me.

12. "Not As I Will"

Blindfolded and alone I stand
With unknown thresholds on each hand;
The darkness deepens as I grope,

Afraid to fear, afraid to hope:
Yet this one thing I learn to know
Each day more surely as I go,
That doors are opened, ways are made,
Burdens are lifted or are laid,
By some great law unseen and still,
Unfathomed purpose to fulfil,
      "Not as I will."

Blindfolded and alone I wait;
Loss seems too bitter, gain too late;
Two heavy burdens in the load
And too few helpers on the road;
And joy is weak and grief is strong,
And years and days so long, so long:
Yet this one thing I learn to know
Each day more surely as I go,
That I am glad the good and ill
By changeless law are ordered still,
      "Not as I will."

"Not as I will": the sound grows sweet
Each time my lips the words repeat.
"Not as I will": the darkness feels
More safe than light when this thought steals
Like whispered voice to calm and bless
All unrest and all loneliness.
"Not as I will," because the One
Who loved us first and best has gone
Before us on the road, and still
For us must all his love fulfil,
      "Not as we will."

13. Doubt

They bade me cast the thing away,
They pointed to my hands all bleeding,
They listened not to all my pleading;
  The thing I meant I could not say;
  I knew that I should rue the day
  If once I cast that thing away.

  I grasped it firm, and bore the pain;
The thorny husks I stripped and scattered;
If I could reach its heart, what mattered
  If other men saw not my gain,
  Or even if I should be slain?
  I knew the risks; I chose the pain.

  Oh, had I cast that thing away,
I had not found what most I cherish,
A faith without which I should perish, —
  The faith which, like a kernel, lay
  Hid in husks which on that day
  My instinct would not throw away!

14. This Summer

I thought I knew all Summer knows,
  So many summers I had been
Wed to Summer. Could I suppose
  One hidden beauty still lurked in
Her days? that she might still disclose
  New secrets, and new homage win?

Could new looks flit across the skies?
  Could water ripple one new sound?

Could stranger bee or bird that flies
  With yet new languages be found,
To bring me, to my glad surprise,
  Message from yet remoter bound?

O sweet "this Summer!" Songs which sang
  Summer before no longer mean
The whole of summer. Bells which rang
  But minutes have marked years between.
Purple the grapes of Autumn hang:
  My sweet "this Summer" still is green.

"This Summer" still, —forgetting all
  Before and since and aye, —I say,
And shall say, when the deep snows fall,
  And cold suns mark their shortest day.
New calendar, my heart will call;
  "This Summer" still! Summer alway!

And when God's next sweet world we reach,
  And the poor words we stammered here
Are fast forgot, while angels teach
  Us spirit language quick and clear,
Perhaps some words of earthly speech
  We still shall speak, and still hold dear.

And if some time in upper air
  One swiftest wings we sudden meet,
And pause with answering smiles which share
  Our joy, I think that we shall greet
Each other thus: "This world is fair;
  But ah! That Summer too was sweet!"

15. January from *Calendar of Sonnets*

O Winter! frozen pulse and heart of fire,
What loss is theirs who from thy kingdom turn
Dismayed, and think thy snow a sculptured urn
Of death! Far sooner in midsummer tire
The streams than under ice. June could not hire
Her roses to forego the strength they learn
In sleeping on thy breast. No fires can burn
The bridges thou dost lay where men desire
In vain to build. O Heart, when Love's sun goes
To northward, and the sounds of singing cease,
Keep warm by inner fires, and rest in peace.
Sleep on content, as sleeps the patient rose.
Walk boldly on the white untrodden snows,
The winter is the winter's own release.

16. February from *Calendar of Sonnets*

Still lie the sheltering snows, undimmed and white;
And reigns the winter's pregnant silence still;
No sign of spring, save that the catkins fill,
And willow stems grow daily red and bright.
These are the days when ancients held a rite
Of expiation for the old year's ill,
And prayer to purify the new year's will:
Fit days, ere yet the spring rains blur the sight,
Ere yet the bounding blood grows hot with haste,
And dreaming thoughts grow heavy with a greed
The ardent summer's joy to have and taste;
Fit days, to give to last year's losses heed,
To reckon clear the new life's sterner need;
Fit days, for Feast of Expiation placed!

17. March from *Calendar of Sonnets*

Month which the warring ancients strangely styled
The month of war, —as if in their fierce ways
Were any month of peace! —in thy rough days
I find no war in Nature, though the wild
Winds clash and clang, and broken boughs are piled
At feet of writhing trees. The violets raise
Their heads without affright, without amaze,
And sleep through all the din, as sleeps a child.
And he who watches well may well discern
Sweet expectation in each living thing.
Like pregnant mother the sweet earth doth yearn;
In secret joy makes ready for the spring;
And hidden, sacred, in her breast doth bear
Annunciation lilies for the year.

18. April from *Calendar of Sonnets*

No days such honored days as these! When yet
Fair Aphrodite reigned, men seeking wide
For some fair thing which should forever bide
On earth, her beauteous memory to set
In fitting frame that no age could forget,
Her name in lovely April's name did hide,
And leave it there, eternally allied
To all the fairest flowers Spring did beget.
And when fair Aphrodite passed from earth,
Her shrines forgotten and her feasts of mirth,
A holier symbol still in seal and sign,
Sweet April took, of kingdom most divine,
When Christ ascended, in the time of birth
Of spring anemones, in Palestine.

19. May from *Calendar of Sonnets*

Month when they who love must love and wed!
Were one to go to worlds where May is naught,
And seek to tell the memories he had brought
From earth of thee, what were most fitly said?
I know not if the rosy showers shed
From apple-boughs, or if the soft green wrought
In fields, or if the robin's call be fraught
The most with thy delight. Perhaps they read
Thee best who in the ancient time did say
Thou wert the sacred month unto the old:
No blossom blooms upon thy brightest day
So subtly sweet as memories which unfold
In aged hearts which in thy sunshine lie,
To sun themselves once more before they die.

20. June from *Calendar of Sonnets*

O Month whose promise and fulfilment blend,
And burst in one! it seems the earth can store
In all her roomy house no treasure more;
Of all her wealth no farthing have to spend
On fruit, when once this stintless flowering end.
And yet no tiniest flower shall fall before
It hath made ready at its hidden core
Its tithe of seed, which we may count and tend
Till harvest. Joy of blossomed love, for thee
Seems it no fairer thing can yet have birth?
No room is left for deeper ecstasy?
Watch well if seeds grow strong, to scatter free
Germs for thy future summers on the earth.
A joy which is but joy soon comes to dearth.

21. July from *Calendar of Sonnets*

Some flowers are withered and some joys have died;
The garden reeks with an East Indian scent
From beds where gillyflowers stand weak and spent;
The white heat pales the skies from side to side;
But in still lakes and rivers, cool, content,
Like starry blooms on a new firmament,
White lilies float and regally abide.
In vain the cruel skies their hot rays shed;
The lily does not feel their brazen glare.
In vain the pallid clouds refuse to share
Their dews; the lily feels no thirst, no dread.
Unharmed she lifts her queenly face and head;
She drinks of living waters and keeps fair.

22. August from *Calendar of Sonnets*

Silence again. The glorious symphony
Hath need of pause and interval of peace.
Some subtle signal bids all sweet sounds cease,
Save hum of insects' aimless industry.
Pathetic summer seeks by blazonry
Of color to conceal her swift decrease.
Weak subterfuge! Each mocking day doth fleece
A blossom, and lay bare her poverty.
Poor middle-aged summer! Vain this show!
Whole fields of golden-rod cannot offset
One meadow with a single violet;
And well the singing thrush and lily know,
Spite of all artifice which her regret
Can deck in splendid guise, their time to go!

23. September from *Calendar of Sonnets*

O golden month! How high thy gold is heaped!
The yellow birch-leaves shine like bright coins strung
On wands; the chestnut's yellow pennons tongue
To every wind its harvest challenge. Steeped
In yellow, still lie fields where wheat was reaped;
And yellow still the corn sheaves, stacked among
The yellow gourds, which from the earth have wrung
Her utmost gold. To highest boughs have leaped
The purple grape, —last thing to ripen, late
By very reason of its precious cost.
O Heart, remember, vintages are lost
If grapes do not for freezing night-dews wait.
Think, while thou sunnest thyself in Joy's estate,
Mayhap thou canst not ripen without frost!

24. October from *Calendar of Sonnets*

The month of carnival of all the year,
When Nature lets the wild earth go its way
And spend whole seasons on a single day.
The spring-time holds her white and purple dear;
October, lavish, flaunts them far and near;
The summer charily her reds doth lay
Like jewels on her costliest array;
October, scornful, burns them on a bier.
The winter hoards his pearls of frost in sign
Of kingdom: whiter pearls than winter knew,
Or Empress wore, in Egypt's ancient line,
October, feasting 'neath her dome of blue,
Drinks at a single draught, slow filtered through
Sunshiny air, as in a tingling wine!

25. November from *Calendar of Sonnets*

This is the treacherous month when autumn days
With summer's voice come bearing summer's gifts.
Beguiled, the pale down-trodden aster lifts
Her head and blooms again. The soft, warm haze
Makes moist once more the sere and dusty ways,
And, creeping through where dead leaves lie in drifts,
The violet returns. Snow noiseless sifts
Ere night, an icy shroud, which morning's rays
Will idly shine upon and slowly melt,
Too late to bid the violet live again.
The treachery, at last, too late, is plain;
Bare are the places where the sweet flowers dwelt.
What joy sufficient hath November felt?
What profit from the violet's day of pain?

26. December from *Calendar of Sonnets*

The lakes of ice gleam bluer than the lakes
Of water 'neath the summer sunshine gleamed:
Far fairer than when placidly it streamed,
The brook its frozen architecture makes,
And under bridges white its swift way takes.
Snow comes and goes as messenger who dreamed
Might linger on the road; or one who deemed
His message hostile gently for their sakes
Who listened might reveal it by degrees.
We gird against the cold of winter wind
Our loins now with mighty bands of sleep,
In longest, darkest nights take rest and ease,
And every shortening day, as shadows creep
O'er the brief noontide, fresh surprises find.

27. The Prince is Dead

A room in the palace is shut. The king
And the queen are sitting in black.
All day weeping servants will run and bring,
But the heart of the queen will lack
All things; and the eyes of the king will swim
With tears which must not be shed,
But will make all the air float dark and dim,
As he looks at each gold and silver toy,
And thinks how it gladdened the royal boy,
And dumbly writhes while the courtiers read
How all the nations his sorrow heed.
    The Prince is dead.

The hut has a door, but the hinge is weak,
And to-day the wind blows it back;
There are two sitting there who do not speak;
They have begged a few rags of black.
They are hard at work, though their eyes are wet
With tears which must not be shed
They dare not look where the cradle is set;
They hate the sunbeam which plays on the floor,
But will make the baby laugh out no more;
They feel as if they were turning to stone,
They wish the neighbors would leave them alone.
    The Prince is dead.

28. A Christmas Symphony

I.

Christmas stars! your pregnant silentness,
Mute syllabled in rhythmic light,
    Leads on to-night,
And beckons, as three thousand years ago
It beckoning led. We, simple shepherds, know
    Little we can confess,
Beyond that we are poor, and creep
And wander with our sheep,
  Who love and follow us. We hear,
If we attend, a singing in the sky;
  But feel no fear,
Knowing that God is always nigh,
And none pass by,
Except His Sons, who cannot bring
Tidings of evil, since they sing.
Wise men with gifts are hurrying,
In haste to seek the meaning of the Star,
In search of worship which is new and far.
    We are but humble, so we keep
    On through the night, contented with our sheep,
And with the stars. Between us and the east,
  No wall, no tree, no cloud, lifts bar.
We know the sunrise. Not one least
    Of all its tokens can escape
Our eyes that watch. But all days are
As nights, and nights as days,
In our still ways.
  We have no dread of any shape
    Which darkness can assume or fill;

We are not weary; we can wait;
  God's hours are never late.
The wise men say they will return,
Revealing unto us the things they learn.
    Mayhap! Meantime the Star stands still;
And, having that, we have the Sign.
If we mistake, God is divine!

II.

Oh, not alone because His name is Christ,
    Oh, not alone because Judea waits
  This man-child for her King, the Star stands still.
    Its glory reinstates,
  Beyond humiliation's utmost ill,
  On peerless throne, which she alone can fill,
Each earthly woman. Motherhood is priced
    Of God, at price no man may dare
  To lessen, or misunderstand.
    The motherhood which came
    To virgin sets in vestal flame,
  Fed by each new-born infant's hand,
    With Heaven's air,
    With Heaven's food,
The crown of purest purity revealed,
Virginity eternal signed and sealed
    Upon all motherhood!

III.

Oh, not alone because His name is Christ,
    Oh, not alone because Judea waits
  This man-child for her King, the Star stands still.

The Babe has mates.
Childhood shall be forever on the earth;
And no man who has hurt or lightly priced
So much as one sweet hair
On one sweet infant's head,
But shall be cursed! Henceforth all things fulfil
Protection to each sacred birth.
No spot shall dare
Refuse a shelter. Beasts shall tread
More lightly; and distress,
And poverty, and loneliness,
Yea, and all darkness, shall devise
To shield each place wherein an infant lies.
And wisdom shall come seeking it with gift,
And worship it with myrrh and frankincense;
And kings shall tremble if it lift
Its hand against a throne.
But mighty in its own
Great feebleness, and safe in God's defence,
No harm can touch it, and no death can kill,
Without its Father's will!

IV.

Oh, not alone because His name is Christ,
Oh, not alone because Judea waits
This man-child for her King, the Star stands still.
The universe must utter, and fulfil
The mighty voice which states,
The mighty destiny which holds,
Its key-note and its ultimate design.
Waste places and the deserts must perceive
That they are priced,

No less than gardens in the Heart Divine.
Sorrow her sorrowing must leave,
  And learn one sign
    With joy. And Loss and Gain
    Must be no more.
  And all things which have gone before,
    And all things which remain,
    And all of Life, and all of Death be slain
    In mighty birth, whose name
  Is called Redemption! Praise!
    Praise to God! The same
  To-day and yesterday, and in all days
    Forever! Praise!

V.

Oh, Christmas stars! Your pregnant silentness,
  Mute syllabled in rhythmic light,
  Fills all the night.
  No doubt, on all your golden shores,
    Full music rings
    Of Happiness
    As sweet as ours.
Midway in that great tideless stream which pours,
  And builds its shining road through trackless space,
From you to us, and us to you, must be
  Some mystic place,
Where all our voices meet, and melt
Into this solemn silence which is felt,
  And sense of sound mysterious brings
Where sound is not. This is God's secret. He
  Sits centred in his myriads of skies,
  Where seas of sound and seas of silence rise,

And break together in one note and key,
   Divinely limitless in harmony!

About AmblesideOnline

This book is one in a series of six, each volume corresponding to the poetry suggestions for Years 1-6 in the AmblesideOnline curriculum.

AmblesideOnline's free Charlotte Mason homeschool curriculum prepares children for a life of rich relationships with God, humanity, and the natural world. Named for the area surrounding Charlotte Mason's schools in England, the AmblesideOnline curriculum is the product of a continuing effort towards a specific vision: to design a course of study that would provide as close a modern approximation as possible of the curriculum created by Charlotte Mason for her PNEU Schools, within the limitations of the current availability of books and materials that match Mason's high standards.

The Advisory, with the assistance of the Auxiliary, lead this work.

The contents of this poetry series, as well as our entire twelve-year curriculum and many other resources, are also available on our website.

amblesideonline.org

Made in the USA
Las Vegas, NV
21 August 2023

76403457R00066